Pomes from a Cow Psychologist

Montana Poetry

Pomes from a Cow Psychologist

Poetry by Mark Forman

Illustrations by Rod Rainey

Edited by Tamara Beardsley-Choat
Design by Candice Forman

About the Cover:

Cover photo of Mark Forman by family friend Jill Hildebrand, taken at the Forman Ranch at Knowlton, Mont., on Feb. 8, 2008. Jill and her husband, Brian, have been much more than just good neighbors — they have been instrumental in helping run the ranch after Mark's death.

And all self-respecting cattlemen and women will understand the importance of the following statement: It should be duly noted, in the event that graphic design should alter the color of the bull, that he is red. Not to be confused with black.

Cover design by Candice Forman.

Back cover illustration by Rod Rainey.

Published by Lavonne Forman.
Compiled by Lavonne Forman, Levi Forman, Jerry and Elaine Forman, and Rod Rainey.
Illustrations by Rod Rainey.
Graphic design and layout by Candice Forman.
Edited by Tamara Beardsley-Choat, Powder River Wild, LLC.

Printed by CreateSpace, a DBA of On-Demand Publishing LLC, a subsidiary of Amazon.com Inc.

To order copies of this book visit:
http://www.pomesbymark.com

Or contact:
Lavonne Forman
HC80 Box 18
Ismay, MT 59336

*Dedicated lovingly to the memory
of Mark A. Forman —
poet, son, brother, husband, dad, rancher,
secretary extraordinaire, friend to so many.*

All of us miss you.

Table of Contents

Acknowledgements

Most projects of this nature require a collaborative effort if all the work and organization is to be accomplished. This one has been done under the additional stresses of grief.

It has been lovingly carried out by a group who wished to see this part of Mark's life preserved and shared. In appreciation we would like to acknowledge the following:

- The many friends and neighbors who inspired us to do a book,
- Mike and Deb Lanthier, whose encouragement went beyond mere words to financial support for this project,
- Jerry and Elaine Forman, for their active interest and contributions to both the content and spirit of the book,
- Rod Rainey for his marvelous art, which lights and enriches the "pomes,"
- Candice Forman for her loving gift of professionally done cover design and layout,
- And Tamara Beardsley-Choat, organizer, motivator, committee chair, editor extraordinaire. Without you this project would still be a pipe dream.

How grateful we are to each of you for the gifts of time, talent and energy you so freely gave to bring this "great idea" to reality.

— *Mark's wife and kids*

Introduction

By Levi Forman

There are two ways it's easy for me to picture my Dad. The first one is outdoors, wearing his dirty and misshapen cowboy hat and his down-filled vest — heading for the big shed or backing his pickup down the hill, filling feed bags or doing any number of other day-to-day ranch things. The other place is at his desk in the basement, tapping away at his typewriter or, more recently, his computer. The tapping of the typewriter or buzz of the adding machine were the sounds I woke to as a child, since Dad and I shared the sanctuary of the basement and the early mornings were when he did his book work.

Dad's office is singularly him and the place in the house where his presence is the strongest. In my mind's eye the room is an interesting combination of chaos and order. Dad never cared much about things looking nice. The office is in an unfinished basement. The bare floor joists that make up the ceiling have all manner of stuff hanging from nails or rolled up and balanced on top of water pipes. The original color of the carpet is hard to determine, and coal dust from the pot-bellied stove that provides what little heat there is in the basement regularly coats everything. If Mom hasn't kidnapped it recently, his coffee cup is guaranteed to have a nice thick coat of brown scum on the inside. I doubt the idea of remodeling ever crossed his mind.

On the other hand, if you open the drawers of the desk or file cabinet, what you find is a wonder of organization. In the desk drawers are a selection of colored pens, each color with a purpose and lying in its own spot in the drawer; various sizes of paper clips and rubber bands, all kept in good supply with replacements ready when they ran out; and rolls of stamps belonging to the different entities he kept books for labeled to keep track of which roll belonged to whom. In the file cabinets hand-labeled folders in alphabetical order contain the records of our ranch, several rural school boards, the Farm Bureau, and various other things Dad kept track of. Nothing is missing, no corners folded over. The names things are filed under are a little unusual to the casual observer, but Dad knew where everything went and everything was in its place. The black 3-ring binder on the desk holds detailed information about all of the cows, the crops, etc. — all carefully printed in his flawless penmanship. On the computer are spreadsheets detailing every bale of hay and every bushel of grain on the place. The register of each of the checkbooks is reconciled to the penny with every bank statement. On the top shelf of the bookcase sit 30 years of diaries, faithfully written every day, the events of each day recorded with dispassionate accuracy and an occasional bit of humor. Hidden in the back of one of the filing cabinet drawers, where once you could have found a bottle of vodka, is an outrageous amount of candy, to be eaten by Dad exclusively.

Dad grew up in the 1950s and '60s in Miles City. Living on the family dairy at the edge of town, he got a taste for both town and country. As far as I know, as a kid he never imagined himself in the cattle business. He had some early aspirations of being a dentist, but eventually went to Missoula to study psychology at the University of Montana, the more liberal of Montana's two universities. Despite the fact that he went to the "hippy school" and worshipped the Beatles and even grew his hair a bit long, it certainly wouldn't have ever been accurate to call him a hippy. His room was a gathering place in the college dorm and some of his fellow students affectionately called him "Dad." He wrote some of his first poems during college and reading these will give you a decidedly different feel than the rest. Due in part no doubt to the professors but also, I believe, to a little bit of teenage angst and anger that you won't find in his more recent stuff.

While Dad was at Missoula, my Mom was in Moorhead, Minn., at Concordia College. They knew each other but only had one date in high school. They started out writing letters and seeing one another when they both came back home for summers and holidays. In 1973, when both had finished their junior year in college, they got married under the pine trees across the road from the house Mom grew up in, which would eventually become their home.

Mom transferred to Missoula for her last year of college, and they lived on campus in married student housing their senior year. Both graduated in 1974 — Dad with a bachelor's in psychology and Mom with a bachelor's in English. I don't know if Dad was disillusioned with psychology at this point or just feeling the pull of the ranch, but he never looked for a job in his field of education. He and Mom moved to the ranch in the summer of '74 and that's where they stayed.

If Dad hadn't planned on being a rancher, he embraced it. Relations between Dad and my grandfather weren't always entirely peaceful, but he never regretted coming to the ranch. My favorite of all of Dad's poems is "I

Ain't No Damn Cowboy," and it beautifully sums up Dad's simultaneous disdain for the glamorous macho cowboy image and his deep love for the life and respect for the people that do it for real.

As much as Dad was a rancher, deep down he was a bookkeeper as well. Perhaps an odd combination, Dad genuinely enjoyed both things. He kept books for Rural School District #38 for over 30 years, and as time went by he kept adding more and more book work, from taking the ranch books from my Grandma Ruthie, to adding more rural school districts, to keeping books for the Custer County Farm Bureau, the Ismay Church, Alcoholics Anonymous and the Knowlton Cemetery. He never got paid much for this — and probably could have gotten more had he asked for it — but it was always more of a hobby than a job for him and he was happy to do it.

Dad combined these two passions, the hard and dirty and somehow profound existence of a Montana cattle rancher and the careful precision of the conscientious bookkeeper, into his art … the poetry in this book. Dad was strictly a rhyme-and-meter kind of poet. One only has to read his "Treatise on Free Verse" to know that he was more into the syllable-counting type of poetry than the "stream of consciousness, drum-tapping beatnik" type. Some people might assume that a lot of these poems leapt from his pen fully formed and delivered by inspiration. But in reality, he worked hard on them, editing them over and over until he was happy with them. He never took them too seriously, he never would have tried to publish them on his own, but he wanted them to be good. Most were written for someone, either on a birthday or a special day, or in some cases (particularly the ones for his brother Jerry or Rod Rainey) to both document and savor a particularly absurd or embarrassing moment in someone's life. Others were serious attempts at art, some of the later of which were edited by Dad's friend and fellow poet, Bob Edwards.

Aside from his work, Dad was a quiet guy. His solitary life on the ranch suited him. Nothing was more miserable to him than being in a big crowd, but he truly liked people on a one-on-one basis. For someone who rarely got further from home than Miles City, and only went there when he had to, both the number and the diversity of his friends is striking. A lot of those friends we only met after he was gone. Be it the recovering alcoholics who shook our hands at the funeral and told us how Dad had helped them. Or the deer hunters who called seeking permission to hunt, and broke down over the phone when they heard the news. Or the people in the offices the ranch does business with, with whom Dad only had an occasional business relationship but still managed to make an impression upon — and who we met only when we visited their offices trying to piece together how all this stuff works, and found folks who fondly remembered Dad and couldn't wait to help us. I believe the only way to collect a group of friends like that is to go through your life treating everyone you meet with respect and friendship, and that's something Dad always did. He wasn't a big talker, but a great listener and a great storyteller. He could sit for hours and trade anecdotes with his friends, and often did.

In his spare time, Dad experimented extensively with all things regulated by the Bureau of Alcohol, Tobacco and Firearms — some of which treated him better than others. He had a love of impractically large handguns and a steady habit of chewing Copenhagen. His relationship with alcohol was fairly brief, and extremely unpleasant, but had a huge impact on his life and enabled him to help a lot of other people going through the same thing later on. For many years he was a passionate fly fisherman, and the annual trips to the mountains were a highlight of every summer. His favorite time of year was fall and winter, the end of hot weather and the frantic pace of summertime on the ranch, and of course the start of the NFL football season. His life contained a good deal of happiness, and like most people, a fair amount of pain and heartbreak. He rarely indulged in self-pity though, and to his last day was grateful for the life he lived.

So we're publishing Dad's poetry. In my mind, these poems are the perfect way to remember Dad — both the guy in the cowboy hat and the guy at the typewriter. If you find yourself with this book, I hope you enjoy it. We didn't print it to make money, just as a tribute to the man we loved and hopefully as a way for more people to get to know him. Or perhaps, for those who did know him, to see a side of him they might not have experienced.

Mark with his first car

Foreword

By Tucker Bolton

"When I was a boy, I would practice my Roy Rogers smile in the mirror."

Mark made this confession to me shortly after we met. We had a common bond in Roy. I knew right then and there Mark Forman and I would be friends. As I enter my sixties I become more aware that all men, regardless of their façade, hold on to a chunk of honesty that can only be found in children. The more of that honesty and wonder they retain, the better the man. Mark had a trunk filled with honesty, wonder and all of the very finest ingredients necessary to whip up this self-effacing, Cowboy Poet that I am privileged to call friend.

Like Tom Sawyer in *Huckleberry Finn*, Mark made me want to be something that I was not. I am not a Cowboy Poet. I spent 50 years of my life as an urban commando in Los Angeles, Denver and Dallas. Mark never held geography against me. He even listened to my poetry and said it was good. Together with other rag tag poets, Jim Russell and Esther Kornemann, we formed the Lower Yellowstone Irregulars. Irregular was the key word. We met three times over a 10-year period. As I composed my epics I would have visions of going to Elko, Nev., rubbing elbows with the likes of Wally McRae and Baxter Black and signing autographs for people with jeans tucked into their twelve hundred dollar boots, turquoise scarves hanging from their necks, wearing shiny belt buckles the size of footballs. I could write about the city and city people. I had survived them both. I could write about sailing the Pacific and foreign ports, as well as my love of the good and bad both had to offer. I could write Cowboy Poetry but I would only do it with my head. That is not enough for poetry. Especially poetry that connects the man with the land and all of the families, people and critters that comprise this vast tapestry that is The West.

Mark Forman is, from the cow stuff on his boots to the greasy sweat stain on his hat, what the West is all about. I had pled with Mark to share more of his work with me. After a considerable amount of time he handed me a brown envelope. Written on the outside was, "Here are some pomes what Mark rote." That evening, after my wife Glenna and I retired for the night, I knew I would never write Cowboy Poetry again. I now knew a cowboy and he was my friend. I woke Glenna with my laughter on a couple of occasions, a tear would roll down my cheek on others. When asked to describe Mark to those that didn't get to know him, my answer has always been the same: "When you look up the word 'gentleman' in the dictionary, there should be a picture of Mark Forman."

In this collection you will learn that being so exhausted that going to bed with "cow stuff" in your ear is a noble option. If you have ever used the words "hick" or "hayseed" as a derogatory term, you may change your mind (I did). You will meet Mark's friends and learn that it's okay to "talk stupid to little animals." Mark even lent humanity, kindness and mirth to those that were inexplicably less than kind.

Lavonne,

Thanks for the best homemade rolls I have ever tasted. Thanks for not being too embarrassed by our getting caught skinny dipping, ankle deep, in the Powder River. Forgive me for having to tear down your fence after sliding down the hill and finding that to be our only way out. Thank you for the first Christmas tree I ever cut myself and the wild turkeys that graced our table. But mostly thank you for the precious time that we got to share with Mark.

— *Tucker Bolton, October 2008*

And Mark, the adventure Gods were still shining on me.

About the "Pomes"

Mark's work stretched over several decades, but in his humble nature, he didn't promote it widely. It was simply his gift to family and friends. His first "reading" didn't occur until Libby Henneberry, the teacher at Knowlton, the local country school, read some of his pieces and asked him to share them at an evening gathering of students, parents and neighbors.

Mark agreed but, although he probably enjoyed it, his intro proves his lighthearted unwillingness to demand attention from his work.

> *"Mrs. H. has asked me to come all the way over here to torture you people with some dumb pomes, and just to show you what poor taste she has in literature, I said I'd do it. She said she wanted me to tell some big windies or do some pomes, and since it hurts my heart to tell a lie, I thought I'd better do the pomes.*
>
> *"Now I suppose I might tell you a little bit about how this all got started. Way back when, I would write a little ditty to go along with birthday cards and such, and I had a lot of fun doing it and some people seemed to enjoy it, so I showed 'em no mercy and just kept on doing it and it finally got completely out of hand and turned into an incurable disease. And now look what happens: Libby hears about it and makes me come over here and make a fool of myself in front of my friends, as some kind of punishment, I guess.*
>
> *"One thing I have never tried to do is to memorize any of my pomes (and that's spelled POMES, not POEMS — there's a difference.) Anyhow, I haven't memorized any, so I have to read them."*

Now the word was out, and on several other occasions Mark was asked to share his work.

He did a couple of readings in Miles City: one at Unique Creations — a local coffee and gift shop, another at Miles City Books and News, as well as one at his 30th high school class reunion. Each time he received rave reviews.

Mark was also asked to share his pieces at the local Ismay Community Church spring banquet in 1996 (appropriately dubbed "The Spring Bawl" in honor of calving season — the primary concern in March among the rancher congregation).

Mark's intro went like this:

> "When Marilyn [May] asked me awhile back if I would do some pomes again, I told her that I didn't have anything new and it would all have to be re-runs (I thought that would get me off the hook). But she said, 'That's all right — do them anyway. We're desperate.'

> "Well, most of you have heard most of these pomes before, and you came back anyhow, which tells me she was right. (We need to get more satellite dishes in this neighborhood.)

> "So here goes the re-runs. If anybody can remember one that they'd like to hear again, just sing out — I've probably got it here. I'm going to pretend that there are some of you that haven't heard these before and tell the story that goes along with the pome — it makes it seem like there's more of them that way.

> "I try to mostly pick on my relatives with these pomes because that's been about the only thing I've found that relatives are good for, and besides that they're all so cruel to me that I'm usually just getting revenge anyway."

Throughout this book, we felt it appropriate to include Mark's comments about specific pomes — many of them written specifically for readings such as those mentioned above — along with the pieces. The stories behind the stories just add to the enjoyment.

— *Ed.*

Oh master of pen, you give me a fit
writing those wonderful words of wit
Write me a few humorous lines
from your cabin set in the pines
Give me the inspiration to sketch a 'toon
"King of the Road". or Man in the moon
Tickle my sides with a stroke of pen
haystack and badger or outhouse and hen
So scribble some lines, you won't regret
This "drawer" is forever, in your debt.

About the Illustrator: Rod Rainey

By Jerry Forman

Rod Rainey, even though not technically related to the Forman family, has been, is, and always will be, a member of our family. Our relationship started out as him being the "kid down the road," who became friends with us as three brothers. That friendship didn't take long to evolve into a strong mutual bond and kinship with the Formans, including Mom and Dad, who looked at him as one of their own kids. He has been through many of the typical family's good and bad times, sharing in those times as more than a friend, but with a commitment that only a family member could devote. From being part of Mark and Vonnie's wedding party, to caring enough to give his all during the horrible times that families sometimes face.

Rod always thought, as did the rest of the family, that Mark should publish his works, but Mark was always too humble to believe they were worthy. On the flip side, Mark and the family always thought that Rod should publish *his* works, but the same thing applied in the humility of the artist. Well, it turns out that we are finally seeing the combined works of these two remarkably talented artists put to print.

Our family has been blessed to have Rod as one of its members for all these years, and we have been graced with his drawings and caricatures that help memorialize various events and places that are special to all of us. I am sure that Mark, even though humble, will look at this book with his "pomes" and Rod's illustrations, and say that it is a great example of what family talent can create.

About the Graphic Designer: Candice Forman

Candice Forman is not only the talented graphic designer behind the cover and inside layout of this book, she is also the niece of Mark Forman.

Candice grew up in Miles City, Mont., the daughter of Jim Forman and Bernadette Skidmore. She graduated from Custer County District High School in 2002, and says a family vacation to Seattle combined with a lifelong love of art lead her to The Art Institute of Seattle. Here she received an Associate of Applied Arts Degree in graphic design in 2004.

After working on the Nordstrom account at Image Mill design and print company for two years, Candice went to work for corporate Nordstrom in 2006, where she currently designs graphics for their private label boys' and mens' lines of clothing.

Candice says she has many fond memories of visiting Mark and Lavonne and her cousins Levi, Luke and Lona at their Knowlton ranch for Easter and Thanksgiving holidays and during the summer. She says her favorite activities there were riding horses and helping gather cattle during brandings. To Candice, her work on this book is a tribute to her uncle and the life he lived.

She currently lives in Seattle with her Persian cat named Leeno.

SECTION: 1

Ballads from the Knowlton Bard

Intro by Lavonne Forman

Webster's Dictionary defines ballad as, "A poem that tells a story of adventure, of romance, or of a hero ... ." In this section of the book you will be treated to the adventures of Rambo Rabbit and the Clank Tank, and visit the lake created when the King of the Road overturns a fire hydrant and the fair is delayed until November.

You will notice that the adventures tend to be misadventures, and the heroes are more accurately categorized as anti-heroes. But then, the purpose of these pomes is not to impress or romance the readers. It is rather to give them the gift of a good laugh and a light and humorous approach to the foibles of life.

Mixed among these comical rhymes are a few serious, thoughtful pieces that show the compassion and respect for life and lifestyle alike of a true rancher.

I Ain't No Damn Cowboy

When people call me "cowboy,"
I just look 'em in the eye
to see if they're insulting me,
and if they are, then why?

To some folks cowboy's just a word
that means that I wear boots
and all that other "western stuff"
that makes up cowboy suits.

To other folks the word implies
I ride a buckin' horse
and swing a curly nylon rope
and bulldog steers, of course.

And then there's them that say the word
with their nose up in the air,
who see a cowboy as a guy
with hayseeds in his hair.

They figure cowboys all smell bad
and spit and say bad words,
and only have the brains it takes
for following cow herds.

Well, hell, I ain't no cowboy then;
if my horse bucks, I fall,
and if I roped at branding
we would NEVER catch 'em all.

Sometimes I ride a combine
and other times I walk;
there's even been a time or two
there was adverbs in my talk.

You're right, I drive a pickup
and I like to take a chew,
but if you think that's "cowboy,"
then I ain't got time for you.

But if your eyes start waterin'
when you see a calf get born,
and if you ever just plain set
with hands on saddle horn,

And if you ever went to bed
with cow stuff on your ear,
and if you've ever waited
for things to come "next year,"

Then you're my breed of people,
you can see the things I see,
and if you name me "cowboy,"
then by God, you honor me.

It's Not Fair

"My favorite victim, er, subject, is my brother Jerry. Most of you know Jerry is the head of the county road department and responsible for the fine roads we have in this county. And just because we have the same last name, it's NOT MY FAULT, I had nothing to do with it.

"A couple years ago, the county crew got trapped into doing a bunch of dirt work at the fair grounds, building a bed to lay some asphalt. They were on a real tight schedule because the fair was about to start, and everything HAD to work perfect. Well Jerry was running a D6 Cat and backed over a fire hydrant, and here came the flood. By the time they got the fire department to get the water shut off, they were just about drowned, and that road bed had to be at just the right moisture content, so they were in trouble."

On a hot July day with the sun beating down,
at the fair was a dozer, on the dozer a clown.
Gouging and digging, kicking dust up galore,
the King of the Road crew said, "Geez, what a bore!"
"I have to admit that this project's revoltin';
I wish I was out spreading gravel at Knowlton,
where those patient poor folks walk to town every day
because ruts big as canyons are blocking their way.
But here I am working on this piddly task;
how 'bout some excitement? That's all that I ask."
So the King of the Road had himself a grand notion:
"Wage war on a fire plug! Create a new ocean!"
Soon, splishing and splashing and squealing with glee,
he cavorted about in the Montana Sea;
he paddled and bubbled and laughed like a nut
till some jerk called a fireman to chew out his butt.
"What the hell's going on here?" the fireman demanded?
The King of the Road had been captured, wet-handed.
His head hung in shame and his feet in the goo,
he felt two-inches-tall, and half-witted, too.
"Just look at this water all over the place!"
the fireman screamed, all red in the face.
"You crawl up on that dozer and act like a cowboy;
you're in a heap of bad trouble right now, boy.
You think you're so smart and you think you had fun,
now take off your hard hat, turn in your grease gun.
But first, you low-down irresponsible pup,
get a great big grease rag, and mop it all up!"

The Heroes

January 1996

"I've got another one starring Jerry and his partner-in-crime and brother-in-law Rod Rainey, who you have to know are the world's two most lackadaisical hunters. They'll plan a hunting trip for a week, and then come out and spend half a day sitting at my kitchen table drinking coffee and telling lies, and then decide it's too late to start hunting, and just go home.

"They came out awhile back, in the middle of the night in the middle of the winter, to what we call the Cummings Place on Powder River, and what they call Mark's Place, in Jerry's old broken-down Dodge pickup, just to hunt rabbits. This one's called 'Heroes.'"

Private First Class Rainey
and Major Problem Grizz
went to Powder River,
to where the rabbits is.
They clumb aboard the Clank Tank
and trundled down the track
to make the nation safe again
from cottontail and jack.
With weapons cleaned and ready
they departed after dark
to wage guerrilla warfare
in the mystic land of Mark.
They patrolled with spotlight blazing,
the enemy was near;
with fingers frozen to the grip
they had their second beer.
In the lonely winter wasteland
the tiny army tramped
until they found the battleground
of Cummings Desert Camp.
There ensued a mighty battle
with screams of pain and hate
until Rod clenched his teeth and said,
"Okay, I'll get the gate!"
In enemy's own country now,
the sweat began to trickle;

if the snack supply ran low
they'd be in quite a pickle.
With clanking stealth they hunted
for their vicious, cunning foe,
the heater turned to "nuclear,"
the radio down low.
When suddenly a rabbit
streaked away across the flat
and Instant-Reflex Rainey said,
"What the hell was that?"
Bazooka smoke soon filled the air,
artillery blasts rumbled,
and out amid the rack and ruin
the hapless bunny tumbled.

In homes across the nation
women knit beside the fire,
the children sleep, and in their dreams
see heroes they admire.
But hardly any know the truth
of why their world's secure,
why their future's clear and bright,
why liberty is pure:
It's all because ol' Rod and Grizz,
two boys not fully grown,
chase Rambo Rabbit half the night
and leave America alone!

The Great Centennial Elk Hunt

"There's another one about these two mighty hunters, who went on a big elk hunt. Their main concern always seems to be whether or not they have enough groceries, and on this trip, Rod thought he was packing the food for both, but Jerry had already thrown in enough for both, too. So while Rod was rationing the supply and starving to death, Jerry knew there was great plenty and was eating like a king.

"On this same trip, they hauled a snowmobile clear up on the mountain, and then spent two days trying to get it running and finally gave up. This one's called 'The Great Centennial Elk Hunt.'"

There once was a couple of rowdy ol' boys
who took to the mountains to make 'em some noise;
They dusted off rifles and loaded their packs
with Twinkies, Korn Doodles, a few Cracker Jacks,
and doo-dads, and whatzits, and thingamajigs,
and parts of dead cattle and most of a pig.
And then while poor Rainey was taking a leak,
Ol' Grizz hid the groceries way down by the creek.
Pretty quick poor ol' Rainey was counting his ribs
while Grizz was all worried 'bout busting his bibs;
But though they both suffered with famine or feast,
their main bugaboo was the John Deere snow-beast.
They wore out their wrenches and used up their cunning
trying to get the ol' S.O.B. running;
They jerked on the rope and they prayed it would start,
but the closest they got was one gaseous fart.
They fought a brave fight but were soundly defeated;
Some dynamite sticks were just what they needed.
So off they went hiking through fog and through snow,
from cloud-covered ridges to canyons below;
They hiked till they dropped — their feet nearly cried;
When Grizz took his boots off, he found his had died;
But not one lone track did they find on their trek,
so back at the pickup they said, "What the heck —
I guess it's a blessing there's no elk today;
We left all our bullets at home anyway!"

American

"Not all my pomes are folklore and history like that one; a few make serious comments on society. This is called 'American.'"

I'm an old-time country boy
a-livin' in the sticks;
The only folks I ever see
are the other country hicks;

But I been watchin' teevee,
and I know just what I lack;
To be a real American,
I need an achin' back.

Or maybe some psoriasis
would bring me up to speed;
with itchy, burning hemorrhoids
I surely could succeed.

If I could get some dandruff
and a pair of bloodshot eyes,
a little gingivitis
just like all them other guys;

a mighty dose of athlete's foot,
arthritis in my knees,
a couple smelly armpits
and a wet and sloppy sneeze,

split ends, toothache,
runny nose,
a touch of constipation,
diarrhea, headache;
I'd belong here in this nation.

I'd be a true American,
and just to reach perfection,
I'd get myself a malady
they call a yeast infection.

But, shoot, I guess it ain't no use,
can't join the brotherhood;
I'm pretty patriotic,
but I'm feelin' too damn good.

Bob

"Once in a blue moon, one of these pomes gets a little more serious. Some of them come from trading some pomes with a friend of mine in Belgrade, who also writes dumb pomes. He sends them down to me to read, and I write him back and tell him how bad they are, and then I send some up to him and he tells me how bad mine are. We are the only two members of what he calls 'The Bad Poets Society.'

"I got a real whiney letter one day griping about the nuts and fruits who live in the Bozeman country, and about the government and the regulations that seem to back up the nuts and fruits.

"Bob is a misplaced country boy who had to leave the ranch for a job that pays real money, but has always dreamed of going back to that life somehow, and it hurts him to see big money folks from back east or from California, buying up ranches without understanding how much it really means to be a part of the land. This one's called 'Bob.'"

My ol' friend Bob fell on his head
and jarred his marbles loose;
it's got him spitting out his food
and swallerin' his snoose.

He rants and raves and carries on
about the damn'dest things,
like wolf hair floatin' in his soup
or spotted owl wings.

He's got to where he just can't see
how kissin' trees is good,
and puttin' diapers on your cow
improves the neighborhood.

He ain't for huggin' buffalo,
he'd never love a ferret;
he ain't for doing anything
that has a touch of merit.

But dig a little deeper,
read the callous on his hand;
you'll see it ain't the critters
that are stirrin' up his sand,

It's all them big-town bureaucrats
who haven't got a clue,
who sit behind the desk and try
to tell him what to do;

And folks who read a bunch of books
and figure they know best
the way us poor dumb yokels
ought to act to save the West.

But follow Bob around some day
and learn just where he's been,
them trees and rocks and buffalo
are just beneath his skin.

You'll never catch him killin' owls
or pissin' in the crick,
and if you say he's hurt the land,
just back up mighty quick,

'Cause he's what "West" is all about,
he honors every part;
an eagle soars between his dreams,
and wolves run in his heart.

Charlie

March 1996

"And for a finisher-upper, I have one that I just put an end on. I don't know if it's really done yet, but I've been pecking away at it for about three years, and it's as done as it gets for now. It isn't exactly a true story, but I sure wish it was. It's called 'Charlie.'"

I never liked that cowboy song
Ghost Riders in the Sky
until one windy winter dawn
when Charlie happened by.

Twenty-four below that day
with wind a-pushin' snow;
the diesel smoke and dusty hay
made all a grayish glow.

Barely light enough to see
the calves along the bunks,
all humped up bowing quietly:
two hundred Buddhist monks.

Then through the snow and smoke and dust
I thought I saw a man;
it rattled me, I thought I must
be drinkin' hard again.

He wore those old-time baggy jeans
and an old four-pocket vest,
he looked just like a photo scene
from the wild and wooly West.

His shirt was buttoned to the top,
his long sleeves gartered down,
side-whiskers cut to mutton-chops
all set to ride to town.

He just stood there and looked at me,
a half-smile on his face;
a cowman come from history
to this exotic place.

It had to be some friend, I thought,
come out to spook me some,
some neighbor yahoo, like as not,
makin' me look dumb;

But then I had to wonder,
just how come he isn't froze,
dressed up like it's summer
in his go-to-meetin' clothes?

Blowin' snow passed through him
without ruffling a hair;
he slowly touched his hat brim
and I saw his hand was bare.

And then I started shakin',
curiosity, it seemed:
just an interested stranger
seeing things he'd never dreamed.

He wandered slowly through the herd
and never spooked a steer,
one by one the critters stirred
from courtesy, not fear.

And when he had 'em all appraised
he looked again at me
and shook his head as if amazed
at what was there to see.

Then he ambled to the feeders
and he signaled me to go,
so I set the scale meters
and threw in the PTO.

And as the wagon rumbled past
he reached out, caught some hay:
I lost sight of him at last
when hay dust blocked my way,

So I bailed out of the tractor cab
and ran back quick's I could
to the far end of the concrete slab
to where the feller stood,

But all I found was melted snow
there on the top fence rail,
and calves all feeding in a row
and the cold wind's lonesome wail.

Charlie's what I've named the guy,
but I'll never know, I guess,
just who the old man was, or why
I feel such peacefulness

Just knowin' he was watchin' me
and might be watchin' now,
and while things change so drastically,
they're still the same somehow.

Makin' Hay While the Sun Shines

It's ninety-five degrees out here,
The sun's a-slamming down,
And up here on this swather
is the hottest place around.

'Cause every single BTU
that old V-8 produces
runs right up my pant legs,
and boils away my juices.

There's forty-seven kinds of bug,
and ev'ry damn one bites;
To them I'm just a Happy Meal
with French-fried hide delights.

Man as Hunter

If you're huntin' in the mountains,
you're gonna freeze your rear;
in fact, some vital body parts
completely disappear!

Wind chills get beneath your clothes
and travel to your brain;
they finally clear the fog away
and you think straight again.

You find this "Man As Hunter" stuff
is nothin' but a sham,
cooked up by some hospital
to get you in a jam;

And then they treat your frostbite
and they send horrendous bills,
and start to talk the next guy
into headin' for the hills.

But you can beat their system
if you're honest with yourself:
just keep the TV clicker near,
leave bullets on the shelf,

Square your shoulders, set your jaw,
make sure it's understood
that from now on you will take pride
in coach-potato-hood!

Minstrels

For Jerry on his birthday

When *Fat & Stupid* roamed the land
in long-forgotten times,
the people came from miles around
to witness tuneful crimes;

They listened with their faces pinched
and finally they cried,
"I don't care WHAT the old song said;
TODAY the music died!"

The boys would pick and strum their way
through hamlets of the West,
gathering their victims
for a tortured music-fest;

And when they got their captives safe
behind the bolted doors,
they'd both take out their weapons
and begin their grisly chores.

They'd murder old-time favorites
and mutilate the new,
they couldn't wait to desecrate
a solemn hymn or two;

The patriotic marching songs
would make the crowd despise 'em,
but mercifully, they played so bad
no one could recognize 'em.

And when the concert ended
it was time to pass the hat,
the boys thought they'd succeeded
if nobody stomped it flat.

Treatise on Free Verse

I heard some "free verse poetry" read on public radio today. I suppose I am going to offend a lot of nice folks who have written some free verse but I have to say what I think.

Free verse is not poetry. The person who writes this string of disjointed thought without going to the Great Bother of paying homage to rhyme, rhythm or meter is beginning from the same place that a real poet begins: a good turn of phrase, a musical bit of the language. But that's all he has. He cannot dredge up the talent to build a poem around the original phrase within the confines of the rules of poetry, so he writes down a long series of basically random thoughts. Free verse is not poetry. Free verse is a story. A very short, pointless, incomprehensible story.

The only way to salvage any dignity after writing some of this drivel is to put a label on it: Art. That word will forever strike terror into the heart of any citizen. When real people hear "free verse," the mind says, "What the hell was that noise all about? It doesn't rhyme, there's no rhythm or meter, it doesn't sing. But they said it's Art. Since it sounds awful and I can't make any sense of it whatsoever, it must really be good, and in order to avoid being called stupid, I should say, 'What a beautiful and significant piece.'" And so the mouth says, "What a beautiful and significant piece."

The only people who really sit down and listen to free verse are other hopeless beatniks who can only write free verse. They can't hold a train of thought long enough to write a story, but they are enamored with their own voices, so they produce free verse, and in order to have anybody sit still and listen to it and say, "Ooh, that's deep," they are forced to endure somebody else's cacophonic renditions and to speak the same words.

I hear the response, which is, of course, "He just doesn't understand free verse." A happy fact for which I will be eternally grateful.

Death on Old Man Creek

Found in Mark's desk drawer, where it was waiting for its final edit.

The little guy was just too small,
he couldn't walk that far;
He'd trailed two miles already
but you know how babies are.

He tried his best to travel
and to keep the herd in sight
Confused and tired and scared and lost,
he still tried with all his might.

So we let the horses part a bit
and the baby dropped behind
We figured that to let him rest
would be a lot more kind.

A couple cowboys headed back
to have a little look,
To see if they could spot the guy,
and find which creek he took.

But what they found on Old Man Creek
was bones and blood and hair,
And coyote tracks that told of how
a life had ended there.

SECTION: 2

Dedicated To

By Levi Forman

These pomes were all written for someone. Left behind on a kitchen table after Dad stopped by when they were out, slipped into some sort of official correspondence, or stuck on a door to surprise then when they got home. They are mostly short and sweet, written on a whim and left behind as a surprise to brighten someone's day.

The fact that you are reading them today, though, shows how much people liked getting them, since they were all saved by their recipients and many years later we were able to collect them for this book.

Trapline

To Griz

I checked my trapline yesterday.
There wasn't nothin' there.
The wind had blown one set away,
and magpies ruined one snare.

I took a shot at one ol' gray
but never touched a hair;
There's jist one thing I gotta say
this trapping is a bear!

P.S.
There was a young critter named Jerry,
as big as a bull, but more hairy.
Some folks call him Grizz,
but the main problem is
that he thinks the name is too scary!

— *Whosis*

P.S. Shave your dog — he sheds like sixty.

THOSE CRAFTY CANINE CRITTERS!

Rhinoceros Stampede

February 4, 2005

I seem to be the victim of Rhinoceros Stampede.
I've got more of the dad-burned things than any man could need.
Just about the time I think they're leaving me alone,
I open up my mailbox: Another one has grown!

My fingers shake, I'm jumpy and I don't sleep well at night
For fear another rhino will come wandering in sight;
But though they keep on showing up and battering my senses,
There still ain't been a single one to make it through my fences.

— *Burma Shave*

*P.S. And I checked out your fence. Next time I need some help building
fence, please go fishing.*

Lousy Day

It would have been a healthy stroll
From Milestown to Knowlton,
And the thought of doing it with kids
Is unbearably revoltin'.

We're Knowlton Family Robinson,
Shipwrecked, tired and crabby;
The bank account is way too tight
To let us call a cabbie.

And then, here comes the hero,
Brandishing his sword
In the empty parking lot
Of Miles City Ford.

But virtue triumphs in the end,
Our hero saves the day;
He fills our hearts with sandwiches
And sends us on our way.

We thank you several hundred times,
There's nothing left to say
You helped to take the ragged edge
Off a really lousy day.

Brothers

This was written for Mark's parents to find when they returned from an extended vacation.

Here I am
and here you ain't;
I'm so lonesome
I might faint.
Us three boys
Have did our best
to bust most things
and smear the rest.

See you Monday
Maybe
MF

River People

For neighbor Deb Burk, who lived on the Powder River
February 11, 1993

The people on the river
are a tough and hardy breed
who live on rock and rattlesnake
and lots of noxious weed.

It's hotter there in summertime,
and often drier, too;
the sun turns up the turbo
to a zillion BTU.

There's forty kinds of bug down there,
and every one has teeth
to eat your ears up topside
and nibble knees beneath.

With all the pain of summer,
is winter their relief?
No way! It's cold as the Antarctic
and never-ending grief.

The snow and ice keep piling up
till their single day of spring,
and then it's all a gumbo mess
that sticks to everything.

This ain't to say there's no good days
when the world's as good as heaven;
I remember well the last one
back in nineteen forty-seven!

Farm Bureau Dues

Written to Curt and Patsy Almy upon being chewed on for no note with their Farm Bureau dues card and pen.

September 26, 1993

I find that it's required, even though I'm old and tired
to send along a witty note when getting dues cards out.
It goes against the grain, but I taxed my tiny brain
to try to find a way to say the things I think about.

It seems to me unjust that some people think I must
compose a lengthy epistle or sonnet or verse
just to complement the pen, while I have to say again:
My poor old head is empty and it's slowly getting worse!

But the only thing most unfair is that you can sit out there
in your mansion in the city where the leisure times accrue,
and all I get, by heck, is a single lonely check
and you even signed the thing without a fancy curlicue!

So in simple black and white: I will never, ever write
a poem or ditty or encyclopedia;
if you want the latest news or some famous feller's views,
you'll have to go and get it from the local media.

So there.

— *Henry Worthless Shortfellow*

To Valorie at 4 Months

January 18, 2001

If the path that you are walking
seems a little bit too steep
and you have to cross some low spots
where the mud gets pretty deep;

If the wind is always in your face
or the sun is blazing hot
and you act sure you can do it
when inside you're really not;

When it looks too big to handle
and some hopelessness sets in
and you stumble to the ground and find
you can't get up again;

You'd like to throw it all away,
admit you've lost the fight
and regain the sad security
of that endless stormy night;

When you think you're finally beaten
and your strength is at the end,
God will pull you up to reach
the shoulder of your friend.

Buck

"I wish I could paint. If I could paint a portrait of my good friend Buck [George], I'd like to paint him just the way I saw him one time maybe fifteen years ago:

"He's sitting on a little shelf of rock along the edge of the Gallatin River. He's wearing a tired out tan cap with sweat stains across the front and halfway down the bill, and a raggedy old jacket with an elbow blown out and a side pocket hanging straight down.

"His back is to the highway and he's not paying any attention to all the cars roaring by; he doesn't know I see him there.

"It's a sunny, cool day with almost no wind; a little halo of cigarette smoke hangs around his head. He's just sitting there, all by himself, real quiet and still. There's a fish pole in his hands, but I've got a notion he ain't fishin', not really. He's just watching that water going by and going by, listening to it talk, and soaking up some peacefulness."

Well, Buck, I guess it's plain to see
that your job here is done.
The second go-round of your trip
has already begun.

Before you leave for good, though,
there's some things you ought to know,
like just how much you've meant to me
these twenty years or so.

You've been a part time Dad to me,
and part time brother, too;
We've traded lies and secrets
and I've shed a tear with you.

I've told you lots of windies,
you named me The Big Liar;
I count that as a compliment
from someone I admire.

You told me when you thought I'd goofed,
and called me Knucklehead,
but there was always caring
in the ornery words you said.

You knew me, all there is to know,
and liked me anyhow.
You're the only "Buck" I've got;
I'm going to miss you now.

These past few years ain't been so kind,
the fun went out of livin';
but all your hurtin's finished up
and every sin forgiven.

So take yourself a breather now,
you've finally earned some rest.
Go on, and meet your Maker, friend,
and soak up peacefulness.

Forman Vet Clinic

FORMAN, ETC. VETERINARY CLINIC
"THE RENDERING PLANT'S BEST FRIEND"
DEATH VALLEY, MONTANA

TO: Mr. Buck George, President
      East Knowlton Cattle, Venison and Coyote Empire
      Ismay, Montana

Charges for miraculous resurrection of two (2) ET calves:	
Hay $60.00?/T ($.037 lb.) 27 days 10/24-11/21 540 lbs.	$ 16.20
Grain little dab	NC
LA 200, first jolt: 22 cc/calf, 12.6$/cc. 44 cc	5.54
LA 200, second jolt, red steer only 22 cc	2.77
Ivomec, both calves, 5 cc. $2.50/dose	5.00
Providing milk cow's calf for company	1.99
Providing milk cow to produce milk cow's calf	675.00
Providing bull to assist with above	1,500.00
Receiving stepped-on foot	.75
2nd time	10.75
3rd time	116.75
Patting backs, whispering, "There, there"	2.66
Night light	1.99
Drink of water, prayers, story, hugs	13.55
Kiss goodnight	7.63
Wiping calf slobber off chin	22.43
Swallowing calf slobber	792.55
Telling calves' story to snoopy Herzogs	13.33
TOTAL CHARGES (PAY UP, BUDDY)	
	$3,188.89

Greetings from Earth

October 9, 1995

I have no words of wisdom,
I'm completely out of wit;
My brains are sore and blistered
From the hours I have to sit.
Trying to come up with rhymes
For that addle-headed Curt;
I scribble out the blunders
until my fingers hurt.
So in the future, Bucko,
Have some mercy on the Clerk:
Just pay your dadburn bureau dues,
Forget about the perks!

— *Henry Worthless Shortfellow*

Hay Status

Last checked hay at 1:00 a.m.

So far have seen no smoke, flame, spark, glowing ember, ash, charred hay, Viet Cong, orangutan, moose, elephant, aardvark, gorilla, sea monster, vigilante, blood-curdling Apache warrior, baby hippo, or 3-legged milking stool, but I did get a fleeting glimpse of a kangaroo with a switchblade.

Careful when you feed.

— Mark (007)

Break Time

If I don't leave a pome today
I s'pose you'll think I'm snotty,
Even though I only came
inside to use the potty —

But makin' rhymes' a lot of work;
If I'd known how hard I'd find it,
I'd have found a bush somewhere
and snuck around behind it.

— *Burma Shave*

Derelict

If things were different in the world
And bad luck never came;
If all of us won lotteries
And all of us had fame;
If nations never went to war
And nobody caught flu
There's one thing that would never change:
You would still be you.
If everything were different,
There's one thing I'd predict:
No matter what went on out there,
You'd be a derelict.

W2 Forms

Sent to Deb Burk with W2 forms
January 8, 1994

I know that you will be upset
if this here form is all you get,
so I'll send a little pome
to liven up your dreary home.

When dark clouds cover up your life
and you feel mired in sticky strife;
the kids are screeching in your ear
and bills are stacked up to your rear;

the pipes are froze, the car is bent,
the mice have found the dryer vent,
the baby trashed the pottery,
you didn't win the lottery;

the telephone is on the blink
and dirty dishes fill the sink,
your husband is a ne'er-do-well;
your life has simply gone to hell.

Just remember all your friends
whose love for you will never end;
It could be even worse, I s'pose —
you *could* have bunions on your nose.

The Ballad of the Morning KATL* Man
(*to be read "cattle")

To Dave Stephen, announcer at Miles City, Mont., radio station
July 1, 1987

On a Monday morning dreary, stubbled cheeks and eyes all bleary
from too much merriment and grog the night before,
the Morning KATL Man comes stumbling, for his keys he's blindly
fumbling'neath his breath he's softly mumbling , grumbling as he finds
the door,"It's just pitiful," he mutters, "having to unlock this door,
     Every day for evermore."

General Bull Moose has the say-so, doesn't like that time of day, so
he sends Dave to do that lonely early-morning chore.
"Be there early," says the Bull, "be sure the coffee pot is full,
and on the air always be cheerful, cheerful's what we pay you for;
what we pay those vast outlandish benefits and wages for,
     Every week for evermore."

Read the rain gauge and the temp, check AP for big events,
who's investigating whom, the endless list of baseball scores;
push the buttons, twist the knobs; the station now begins to throb
as Dave the Morning KATL Man does the jobs he can't ignore:
the myriad eternal jobs he's done a million times before,
     And will again, for evermore.

All around him folks are sleeping, as the sunrise, gently creeping,
brings to life the world of bugs and birds once more. Groggily he clears
his throat; he sounds just like a nanny goat who swallowed parts of
Granny's coat, the wool one hanging by the door. A voice of dust and
rust and wool, not what the town is list'ning for:
     A cheery voice for evermore.

One more dose of coffee grounds pulls his scratchy voice around
to sound more like the Morning KATL Man of yore;
one last check of knob and dial, he's ready now to talk awhile,
to rouse the sleepy town from that last drowsy moment we adore;
he helps the groggy countryside get its feet upon the floor,
> And will again, for evermore.

— With sincere apologies to Edgar Allan Poe
from The Bard of Knowlton

Limerick to The Bard

By Dave Stephen

A. B. C.
MUTUAL · INTERMOUNTAIN
AFFILIATE

Box 700
MILES CITY, MONTANA

To... THE BARD

From... NNS

Subject... RHYME & METER

Date... 7/13/87

A PLAGERISTICAL POET NAMED FORMAN
WOULD PEN A BAD RHYME AND SAY "OH, MAN!
I KNOW ITS A SIN
WHAT I DO WITH MY PEN
BUT THE FAULT'S JUST HALF MINE, SO STOP GROANIN'."

Letter to Dave Stephen

July 16, 1987

An announcer I once found appealing
has crudely accused me of stealing.
Now I'll go to my grave
with ill will for the knave,
and my heart will be years in the healing.

Dear Sir:

I take instant and unbridled offense at the idea that my masterpiece
could be considered plagiarism. Destruction of property, maybe, or
desecration of art, but plagiarism?! Indeed!

Actually, it was kind of a relief to realize that copyright laws and such
wouldn't allow you to mention the thing on the air. As soon as I put it
in the mail, I got to thinking about the fact that I had put it together
for the entertainment of ol' Dave, and about the jillions of listeners
who knew nothing about poetry except that they didn't like to study it
in high school, and had probably never even heard of Edgar Allan Poe,
much less "The Raven," and I began to wish I hadn't sent it without a
"Private and Personal" heading. Anyhow, thank you for the
limerickical reply, and "plagiaristical" is not, never has been, and never
will be a word.

Keep up the good work, and thank you for your support (I suppose
you'll call that plagiarism, too).

Best wishes,

Mark Forman
President
Dave Stephen Fan Club

The Explanation

January 22, 1993

I came to town and used your car;
I don't know where the hell you are.
But if you fail to hide your keys
in circumstances such as these
You'll find it used by some poor bloke
who's in town 'cause his window's broke.

He's tired of all the winter air
that settles 'round his derriere;
He's tired, too, of lunches that
Got ate up by the gol-durn cat;
There's lots of things to gripe about
since he knocked his window out.

I tossed some firewood in the air
and where it fell I knew not where;
At least until I heard the "klunk"
of firewood landing in the junk
that cluttered up my pickup bed;
Then, something made me turn my head
to see, to my complete dismay
A sight that haunts me to this day:
The wood, as if possessed by demons,
Propelled by devil's evil schemin's
Took one huge athletic hop
And even though I screamed, "No, STOP!"
It soon reposed, 'midst broken glass
Right where I usually park my ass.

Bear Cares

For Pa
December 2002

When wandering in the wilderness
and you come across a bear,
Think about the twist of fate
that put you both right there.

"What are all the forces
that have made me who I am?"
In the meantime he will eat you,
'cause he doesn't give a damn.

Through the Pain

This very day the dentist drilled me,
the pain and agony 'bout killed me,
but boundless courage pulled me through
so I could write this poem for you.

Cold Pop

I looked for a Coke
but I only found Shasta —
Guess a guy settles
for whatever he hasta —

I twisted the nose
of the ol' thermostat
and in front of the
heavenly breeze I done sat.

With my blood finally cool
and my brained turned to jelly;
a can of that yucky ol' pop
in my belly,

Renewed once again,
I think the same thought —
"Why does it have to get
so stinkin' HOT!?"

Hate it, hate it, hate it.

— *Burma Shave*

"THANK GOD FOR A LONG SHIRT TAIL"

As you sit and ponder
Your mind away off yonder
Doing your job you grunt & groan
All alone on your morning throne
The world is all but yours
To organize the morning chores
The aroma getting a wee bit strong
Maybe you've been sittin a might too long
But your job is caught up short
Your mission you must abort
Two hunters dressed in blaze
Barely see them thru the haze
Stand in the doorway to request a hunt
A furry Grizz and a scrawny runt

Eyes watering from the smell
You tell them both to go to hell
Their heads hanging a bit askew
Toilet paper stuck to their shoe
You feel for a moment, a little weak
And tell them to hunt down the creek
Their spirits lift & off they poke
In a blue Dodge Klunk, what a joke
You look down all white & pale
Thank GOD for a long shirt tail!

Smile — You're on Candid Pencil!

Written as a re"butt"al to Rod's poem and illustration.

You'd think a guy could settle down
and sit upon the pot
without the whole world coming 'round
and bugging him a lot.
But not while Rainey's in the house;
you're not safe anywhere:
that mangy weasel and his mouse
will come a-peeking there.
He caught me in my favorite pose
with my britches 'round my boots,
solving all the world's woes
while tooting smelly toots.
So, when Mother Nature calls,
be sure you go prepared:
wear a shirt that hides your balls
and for God's sake, comb your hair!

SECTION: 3

A Gift of Words

By Jerry Forman

I am sure that I can speak for anyone, family or friend, when I say that the best gift Mark could ever give someone was a card with a little "pome" written in it. Along with taking the time to find the goofiest card for the occasion, he would almost always write something that made fun of the person getting the card.

His pen had no shame when it came to telling you how little hair you had, or reinforcing the fact that as we were getting older, our minds and bodies were failing miserably. That was the thing that was the best though. No matter what he wrote, everyone wanted to read what was in the card, and those who he wrote about knew without a doubt, that the more he made fun of them, the more he showed the affection and love he had for them without getting "mushy."

Mark didn't do mushy, that was good because I think we all felt a little more special when he picked on us. Even Mom was not safe from his wit, even though he was a little kinder to her than most people. He was usually extra kind at Mother's Day, and would write something to make her feel proud to be his mother.

I don't know how most people do things, but I'm sure a lot of people don't hang on to birthday cards or the likes for very long. This book however, is a testimony to what a precious gift he gave us, that we would keep his writings for this many years. (Mark would slap me if he heard me call his works "precious.")

We all love him, and will miss those special occasion cards, and cherish the ones we have.

No Wonder

To Mom on Mother's Day
1992

I often used to wonder why
Mom was always there to try
to soothe the hurt and ease the pain
for nasty kids, who, it was plain
would never thank her for her work,
and would always be a jerk.

Now I'm older, and I see
some answers to the mystery
of why the geese go south each fall,
why moss is short and trees are tall,
why the bird said, "Nevermore,"
and what my belly button's for.

But I will never comprehend
how a mother could defend
that monster that a kid can be,
and do it always thanklessly:
as often as a mom gets stung,
no wonder some things eat their young.

Three-Quarters Kid

For Ma on Mother's Day

When a feller's pushin' fifty
and his hair is turning gray;
when he's s'posed to fret and worry
about things to do today —

When he should be all adult-ish
and think adult-ish thoughts
about the ozone layer
and the bombs that Russia's got,

or the future of the country,
civic duties and the like,
or the ever-present danger
of another interest hike …

But I don't have to grow up yet,
take blame for things I did:
Long's a feller's got his mom,
he's still three-quarters kid!

The Parts Man

1993

"Most of you know my brother Jim who is the part manager at Horizon Equipment. Awhile back Jim turned 39, and was complaining about being "OLD" and complaining about being the eternal parts man, so I sent him this heartfelt expression of my sympathy."

Picture this inside your head:
Gray hairs drifting to the floor,
most the brain cells sick or dead,
bearings that won't bear no more.

Gears and sprockets worn to points,
springs no longer spring,
creaks and groans in all the joints,
and rust on everything.

Upholstery cracked and worn so thin
the stuffing's showing through:
Be sure and take your vitamin,
and grease the babbitts, too.

It's probably too late to save
this broken-down machine;
it's got one axle in the grave
from all the wrecks it's seen.

But cheer up — you can buy a part:
replace the one you broke;
they even have a plastic heart
or a universal yoke.

It might be six or seven years
before you have to see:
There ain't, it sadly now appears,
no lifetime guarantee.

Not Better, Just Older

When you wake in the morning,
your hinges all creak;
your wife sees your face
and she eeks a big "EEK!"

You're grumpy and growly
and ready to snap
at kids who all scramble
to climb on your lap;

Your belt's a bit tighter,
your boots farther down,
and renting a movie's
your night on the town.

Days seem to be longer,
the cold ones are colder:
You ain't getting better,
you're just getting older!

Happy Birthday, you mangy ol' scoundrel.

— *Mark & Co.*

Questions of Age

For Jerry's 33rd birthday
1993

A third of a century, thirty-three years
makes a man think about some of his fears:
Can I finish projects, once I've begun 'em,
and if the girls chase me, can I outrun 'em?

What if some space junk falls down on my head;
will I have a headache, or will I be dead? And if dead,
will I land on my back or my face,
will I go to heaven or some other place?

What if an Ice Age takes over next week,
will my fingers get numb so I can't take a leak?
Will I wet my pants or rupture my bladder?
(Can't think of nothin' that makes me much madder.)

And what if an elbow grows out of my throat,
and what if my mother turns into a goat,
how 'bout if Montana secedes from the land,
and what if a bumblebee sits on my hand?

When a guy finally reaches the big thirty-three,
life gets pretty complicated, you see;
but one thing oughta scare you a little bit more:
the questions get dumber at age thirty-four.

Fishing for Thoughts

Ralph's Birthday
1992

When the sunshine hits the river
And wakes up the salmon flies,
It makes a feller quiver
And begin to fantasize:

He knows the name of every trout,
He sees where each one hides
Before he gets his fly rod out,
Runs leader through the guides.

The best part of existence
Is the planning and the dream;
Before we meet resistance
And before we reach the stream.

So on your birthday, here's my wish:
I hope you'll keep on dreaming,
And if you NEVER catch a fish,
You'll limit out on scheming.

It's Your Day

Lavonne's Birthday
1994

Though kindergarten has you down
and Christmas has you frantic,
the world is crumbling 'round your ears,
the list of bills gigantic;

There's ribbon in the cookie dough
and tinsel in your hair,
you check your energy reserve
and find there's nothing there;

Lean back and know today's your day,
slack off and take a breather;
you don't have to sweep the floors
or wash the dishes either;

Forget about your cares and woes,
the misery and sorrow,
you can bet no matter what,
they'll all be back tomorrow.

Jim

To Mark's brother Jim on his birthday
May 12, 1996

I know that it's my duty
and it's time to pay the price:
An older brother must give out
a lot of good advice.

If you don't pay attention
and go spittin' in the wind,
you'll find you've got some gooey stuff
a-hangin' off your chin.

Or if you're goin' huntin'
at the very crack of dawn,
you gotta be real careful when
you put your britches on.

If you tug 'em on and find
the zipper is behind you,
the ankles are a little snug
and somehow they just bind you,

It's time to turn the light on
and get set to face the facts;
you'll find out what your wearin' is
the wife's new paisley slacks!

Jerry

To Mark's brother Jerry on his birthday

You get up in the morning
and you're grouchy as a boar,
Your joints all ache a little
and your head hurts even more.

The reason for your bad mood
before you reach the door:
the world ain't getting' worser
You're just pushing twenty-four.

— *The Knowlton Hillbillies*

Your Star

Written to Levi for his high school graduation
May 1995

A dozen years completed
(and with just a few repeated),
now you're set to go in debt
(expletive deleted).

You thought it was revoltin'
you'd be stuck so long at Knowlton;
the senior high had caught your eye
and you just started moltin'.

You left the country school behind
to go and see what you could find
and stepped into a life of new,
and old, somehow combined.

So now you take another pace,
you almost recognize the face;
begin to see the man you'll be,
and the boy that he'll replace.

Carry with you all you are,
but don't be scared to wander far;
you hold the deed to all you need;
just reach, it really IS your star.

— *Author Unknowin'*

Ornery Coot

For Ralph on his birthday
1994

Most say that Ol' Ralph is an ornery coot,
A devious devil, a villainous brute;
With wild stringy hair and one cancerous eye,
I'll have to admit that he's one scary guy.

His long yellow fangs and nose off to one side
Will make little children scream once and then hide;
His back has a hump and his hands look like claws
When he clutches the animal bones that he gnaws.

He pulls wings off flies and throws cats in the mud
And it's rumored he ain't even too scared of blood;
One leg has been broken, he walks with a hitch,
His laugh is a cackle that sounds like a witch.

He lurks in dark alleys or under thick hedges
Or up in tall buildings, outside on the ledges;
He'll glare at a cop or the poor meter maid,
Slow down when in front of a truck on a grade;

He spits on the sidewalk, he won't wave at trains,
Won't change his shirt though it's covered with stains;
He thumbprints the mirror, he leaves the lid up,
Won't even talk stupid to kittens or pups.

But I know him better, see through the façade,
I know that he's not irredeemably flawed;
Though most people think he's a hopeless old goat,
I can say this for him: he's got a nice boat.

Life

We all get old and fall apart,
machinery squeaks and squeals;
pills for belly, spleen and heart
are highlights of our meals.

The mind becomes a deadly foe
that thinks up crazy things,
forgets the stuff we need to know
and spends time wandering.

The joints and muscles hurt till noon,
the ears don't hear so good,
eyes will need trifocal soon,
fingers don't work like they should.

But as we age, it seems to me,
priorities keep changing;
Vital stuff that used to be
is slowly rearranging.

We've lifted all we need to lift,
we've run as hard as needed;
now we receive the real gift:
knowing we succeeded.

But don't be figuring you're through,
your mission ain't complete:
those of us who follow you
need help as WE compete.

Old Fart

Ralph's birthday
1990

If you need a way to celebrate
the seventh of December,
Come on out and run a gate
(a skill you'll soon remember).

We'll give the calves a zillion shots
And get kicked upon our knee;
All covered up with poop and snot,
We'll leap about with glee.

With any luck we'll freeze our buns,
a-sloshing through the snow,
having lots of winter fun
as up the chute we go.

Or if you want, just sit right here
And skip the chilly part,
I'll bring you in some birthday cheer
And call you "an old fart."

Untimely

Written in a "late" birthday card for Mark's mother, Lanie Forman. Lanie and Ralph normally spent the winters in Phoenix but this particular year, they didn't go.

January 4, 1993

I know you'll think this card is late
and I'm a shiftless reprobate
for never doing things on time
(or doing them in corny rhyme),

but think about it just a sec
before you try to wring my neck;
cut me just a little slack
before you start the big attack.

My calendar is all a mess
because of your untimeliness:
on most years' January thirds
you're down south with the gooney birds.

Now I think it's still December,
lots of time left to remember;
I usually think about your card
first time I see your empty yard,

and then I think, "Oh, what the heck,
we'll have some kind of postal wreck
and she will never get my card:
there ain't no use in trying hard."

So if this wish is not on time
it's definitely not my crime;
you've thrown off my entire year,
it's not my fault that you're still here.

But Happy Birthday anyhow,
I hope you had a jolly WOW,
and if you want revenge some day,
just send my card in early May!

Downhill

Your whiskers have now turned to gray,
your skin is wrinkled up;
Your joints all creak at break of day
with your second cup.

Your arteries are lined with crust
and ashes fill your head,
your love life is a total bust:
You might as well be dead.

Remember through the pain and strife
while you're crying in your beer;
this is the best day of your life;
It all goes downhill from here.

— *Mark & Stu*⊠

Forty

We couldn't let this day go by
Without a stupid verse
Commemorating forty years
For better or for worse.

You didn't want a party,
So we'll just stay home and pout;
Now you don't have anything
To cuss your kids about.

But even though there's no balloons,
No streamers and no crowd,
This is a most momentous day
And all of us are proud.

Giving up and getting out
Seems to be the way
That people solve their problems
And get along today.

Forty years is quite a spell
To keep on keeping on,
But we're guessing it was worth it,
Because neither one is gone.

Congratulations to you both
For surviving all the troubles;
Here's hoping that for forty more
The jolly times will double.

And speaking of that forty years,
It takes eighty now, you know,
To get your names immortalized
On the noon Paul Harvey show.

Go for it.

Past Prime

For Ralph's birthday
1995

Well, here's another birthday;
s'pose I gotta write a rhyme
to glorify the birthday boy
before he's past his prime.

I suspect I better hurry
or the prime might pass me by
like shootin' stars that disappear
in the blinking of an eye.

But then I get to thinkin':
your prime ain't just one day;
it can be a flowing thing
if you work it the right way.

if you believe you're better
than you were a year ago,
if you've got a goal or two,
some rows you're gonna hoe,

If there's stuff you want to learn
or places left to see,
there's a new prime every minute,
and you're in it, constantly.

Leaving Knowlton School

For Luke on his 8th Grade Graduation from Knowlton School

Now Lucas is leaving the old Knowlton School;
He walks away knowing he's nobody's fool;
He's suave, debonair, unbelievably cool
And darn near as pretty as Festus's mule.

He's king of the mountain here, top of the heap,
He hurdles first-graders in one mighty leap;
He spouts all his wisdom and piles it on deep
Until sometimes the little kids think he's a creep.

When he gets to the city he's gonna find out
That somehow he's lost just a bit of his clout;
Upperclassmen will teach him, I haven't a doubt,
What being a scumsucking freshman's about.

But that's just their job, to put freshmen down,
Time-honored tradition passes on like a crown:
When you deal with a freshman, you MUST wear a frown
And treat him like he's just an out-of-town clown.

When the first shock is over, I'm sure he will see
That Knowlton has helped him be what he can be;
He'll stand with the best, toe-to-toe, equally,
And show 'em our country-style high quality.

So we wish him the best and we tell him we're proud
To have him represent us in that urban crowd;
Just have fun and do what by law is allowed,
And STAY OUT OF PRISON, for cryin' out loud!

Growning Up

For Grizz

There comes the day in each man's travels
the mystery of life unravels;
your problems start to fall in place,
and with new confidence you face
each trial as it comes your way,
living life from day to day.

Your mind looks farther forward now
and farther back: it seems somehow
your world is not just "right this minute"
and your future and your past are in it;
and every day you're getting bolder,
but that's not just from getting older ...
It's from growning up.

— *Henry Worthless Shortfellow & family*

Geezerhood

Written for Mark's dad, Ralph, on his birthday
2003

When taking off your boots at night's
the highlight of the day
And you're really looking forward
to when you can hit the hay.

When nights out are like punishment
(You'd skip 'em if you could)
You know you've reached the summit:
You achieved your Geezerhood!

Geezerdom

For Ralph
December 20, 2003

If you think you're getting older
and your blood is running colder,
Why not take a little bolder
look at what your life's become.

If the joints are stiff and creaky
and the memory is leaky
and you've gone to using sneaky
ways to get your own way some;

Just remember you're forgiven
for no longer being driven
for the slower life you're livin':
You've accomplished Geezerdom!

True Romance

Lavonne's birthday
1993

Another birthday comes along when things are really frantic,
and then I try to find something that kinda seems romantic;
I find that as romance, I would make a darn good plumber,
'cause every single plan I get seems just a little dumber.

You need some kindergarten clothes that should be armor-plated,
and you think your party duds are getting kind of dated;
but if I pick out clothes for you, you'd stir up quite a scene:
what I would pick would prob'ly be just right for Halloween.

Does yellow go with polka-dots, if all the stripes are thin?
And is it true that slack are out and mini-skirts are in?
Are hiking boots accepted if the dress is long and formal?
Is wearing Day-Glo leotards considered too abnormal?

It might just work out better if you pick the stuff yourself;
maybe that way it won't end up on St. Vincent's shelf.
So here's a gift certificate that's good at any store,
but there are some restrictions as to what it's valid for:

It will not work for groceries or for stuff like rug shampoo,
it's only good for clothes, you see, and ONLY clothes for you.
It isn't too romantic, some would say it's lousy taste,
but I searched my brain and all I found was putrid toxic waste.

Happy Birthday

— *Meager Allen Poet*

Thirty-Nine

Thirty-nine years and you're still going strong,
Kicking and gouging and fighting along;
Long years of passion and struggle and strife
As a grumpy ol' husband and crotchety wife.

You got through the good times as well as the bad
And now you've forgotten the doubts that you had;
You look at yourselves and you think all is fine;
You're ready to start on the next thirty-nine!

Not Grown Up Yet

Dad's 64th birthday
1993

Gadzooks, methinks another year
Has stealthily crept by;
A multi-candled birthday cake
Now looks you in the eye.

But wield thy trusty sword, brave knight,
And fend off middle age;
You've fought a lusty fight so far —
Resist that frightful stage.

You can't recover eagle-eyes
Or perfect hearing, either;
You don't quite make it up the hill
Without a little breather;

Your hair is thinning just a bit,
Your teeth are in a cup;
But thinking's the important thing,
And yours ain't near grown up!

Age

Jim's birthday
2002

When your aches & pains assail you
and your muscles start to fail you,
just remember all the wisdom
in this little birthday verse.

You can fight it like a demon,
you can face it kickin', screamin',
but the clock will keep on ticking:
it will steadily get worse.

But you'll find some satisfaction
(in your life of slower action)
in knowing that you'll get to ride
in Stevenson's white hearse.

In the meantime, keep on living,
grab whatever life is giving;
you can take away the power
of the dreaded mortal curse.

Nearly Dead

Jerry's birthday 2000

Well, scratch your pore ol' balding head
and think about the things I said:
Each birthday brings you mounting dread;
with forty-one, you're nearly dead
And if your sanity has fled
and if you're soon to become wed,
just wander off with weary tread,
lie down and go to sleep instead.

High Hopes

Father's Day
1985

I haven't wrote no poems for you;
My brain had gone to sleep.
Although you hoped all winter through,
From me there weren't a peep.

So now it's time to make amends
And rhyme a line or three,
So once again we can be friends
And you won't gripe at me.

Two things I hope will come from this
(would give me quite a thrill):
to get back on the Christmas list
and maybe on the will.

But even if I'm not forgave,
There's this I want to say:
Be loyal, kind and true and brave,
And Happy Pappy's Day!!

Getting Old

Ralph's birthday
2000

When your knee has given out
the morning jog you'll do without;
and when your heart runs off and on
you must forego the marathon.
If your ears don't hear so good
and words aren't always understood,
your memory has failed you some
and kids these days have gotten dumb;
just know you must have reached that stage
that's almost into "middle age."
So now it's true, it must be told,
Look out, you might start getting old.

Finding You

To Lavonne on Mother's Day
1993

I wish I knew a way to say
(without it sounding sloppy)
that having you to raise my kids
has made me very hoppy.

There's been a time, or maybe two,
I've been "Best Dad on Earth,"
but I'm usually grouchy outside
and selfish undernearth.

The kids need someone patient
and that's one thing I ain't,
but they've always got their mama
who can do the things I cain't.

They need someone forgiving,
who will say, "Oh, what the heck,"
while I would usually throw a fit
and wring their scrawny neck.

So anyhow, I thank you
for doing what I cain't:
finding you to raise my brood
was a lucky accident.

College Invention

For Levi on his birthday
April 16, 1996

When you're basking in the sunshine
on the green lawns of DeVry,
watching fluffy clouds and life
go slowly drifting by;

Think about your relatives
a-calving in the slop
and getting sad-eyed faces now
from wishing it would stop

the endless winter cycle
of snow and freeze and blow,
and then warm up for two short days
before another go.

We've paid our dues, we've done our part,
we've finally had enough;
so build a weather-fix machine
and please delete this stuff!

Ambitions

To Mother on Mother's Day

You got one kid who fixes roads
And one falls off his horse,
Another peddles John Deere stuff
(all overpriced, of course).

You figured on a lawyer
Or a doctor or a priest
Or maybe even president;
A senator, at least.

But when we moved away from home
And left you standing on the stoop,
We sallied forth upon our own
And became three nincompoops!

Paybacks

For Ralph

Don't wanna write a poem today,
My brain is standing still'
But if I don't, there's hell to pay:
I'm scratched right off the will —

So here's a little ditty
For Pa, although it's late;
I know it isn't pretty
But hey, let's celebrate!

Years of grief and sufferin'
And trying to be wise
Result in three old ruffians
Who never sympathize.

Instead of being grateful
For all the things you did,
They bum another plateful
And *you* babysit their kid!

Purty

To Jim on his 30th Birthday

Although you're feeling purty,
just remember what I said:
Once you get past thirty,
you might as well be dead.

The Only Thing

1992

A mother holds her newborn babe
and pictures such idyllic scenes
of trophies, thrills and accolades
and rainbows made of jelly beans.

Graduations, proms and such,
doctors, lawyers and the like,
senators and presidents,
a little tiny, squeaky trike,

First step, then the wedding march,
a scholarship from M.I.T.,
shining eyes and curly hair,
the Nobel Prize, or two, or three!

What surprises lie in store:
one leaps to crack his head,
and Mother's cheeks flush rosy at
some thing the youngest said.

They're on the "ten most wanted" list,
fly kites next to a power line
they tear off "Don't Remove This Tag"
they burp out loud each place they dine.

But saint or sinner, genius, fool;
to Mom, they're all first place,
and that's the only thing that's saved
this crazy human race.

Lucky

For Lavonne

I'm having trouble writing
'cause I've said it all before,
but I can say it once again
and mean it even more:

I love my kids with all I have
but sometimes that's too small
I'm often too wrapped up in me
to be any good at all —

But you have always been there
to do the lion's share,
to put them first like they deserve,
each time, and everywhere.

They've been lucky, so have I
for the anchor that we've had
so we can make our big mistakes
and it don't turn out too bad.

SECTION: 4

The Long-Haired Years

By Lavonne Forman

Reading this section of the poetry makes me smile. I remember the young man who took this writing so seriously. He wrote faithfully, at least a little every day. A lot of what I knew about Mark in the early days of our courtship came to me in daily letters from Missoula, as he developed his craft and found his voice. He took lots of writing classes but his favorites, as I remember it, were with Dr. Hugo where he learned to write poetry and received many kudos for his efforts.

Although his hair only stayed long for a semester or so, calling them the long-haired years is correct. It was a time when he thought through a wide range of philosophy and life-styles before settling down to the life we both loved so much. That time left traces in him for all of his life. He had a broad acceptance of the wide world with all of its diversity. It was expressed in the diversity of his friends and the classical music he usually played in his pick-up while he was feeding cows or doing any of the thousands of ranch jobs that he also loved. He just never could be a stereotype. I hope you will enjoy a brief visit to the mind of the man I fell in love with in 1972.

— *Vonnie*

Warm Springs, Montana

Old man kept a doorknob
hanging on a string
from the ceiling
in his bedroom.
Pretended it was his wife,
who kept a doorknob
hanging on a string
from the ceiling
in her bedroom.
Pretended it was her husband,
who kept a doorknob.

Bullbat

A bullbat ain't.
A bat, that is.
He's a nighthawk.
But he's not like
A hawk, neither.
He only flies at night,
Or dusk, or when you
Scare him up from
A sagebrush by day.
Then he flies a ways,
And finds another brush
And hides again.

Coffee

I've got a cup here full of crap
That used to taste like coffee,
But now it's cold and bitter black;
Forgotten, wasted. When I came back
I found it like a glass of lacquer
Sitting, waiting, smelling dead.

The telephone had sent me off
To things that were important.
A cup of coffee doesn't count;
Won't matter, won't amount to much;
I'll dump it in the sink, I think.
Instead, I hold my breath, and drink.

Saturday Matinee

A marching-music John Wayne war
filled with technicolor gore
and blood & guts & guns & more:
generals wearing shiny boots,
soldiers who don't forget salutes,
and two krauts die when John Wayne shoots —
that's what those good guys are for.

Coke and popcorn, Hershey bars,
boo the bad guys, cheer the stars
as they go collecting battle scars.
Wave your arms and stamp your feet
when the enemy admits it's beat —
these movie shows are really neat.
Outside, a hundred moms, in cars.

Two Poems About Uncle Gordy Who Was Dead in Jamestown, North Dakota

1. Ten thousand flowers, aluminum box,
   Teflon skillet for Margarine Man,
   remembering tight-faced the time
   he hit his thumb with a hammer.

   Knock on forehead, see if he's home or
   in a bar in Texas.
   Lift fingers — do morticians really
   steal belt buckles?

   I tried to teach him to fly-fish once,
   He taught me to shoot scattergun.
   I can't shoot, he can't fish.
   No one will ever write a poem for you, Uncle Gordy.

2. Jamestown, North Dakota is a good place to be dead.
   Dead is a good thing to be in Jamestown, North Dakota.

Gray Sidewalks

Hands fisted loose
in my pockets, I
wonder, wander
afoot, alone;
attracted to houses
who have no friends
or lovers;
no ends
or beginnings;
no sins or secrets
or paint.
Drab, drab, drab.
On the poor side
of town.

The Chicken

With deepest apologies to Edgar Allan Poe:

Once upon a noontime weary, in the outhouse rank and **dreary**,
I sat in contemplation deepest of comic heroes I adore.
While I posed in ope'-mouthed wonder, suddenly there came a thunder,
As of some explosion under, underneath the reeking floor.
" 'Tis some truck outside," I muttered, "rumbling past my outhouse door
           — Only this and nothing more."

Ah, distinctly I remember it was the hot September
And the outhouse cooked and simmered under ruthless summer sun.
Work had forced me here to hiding — no longer could I stand the chiding
Of my boss who lived for toil and recognized no need for fun;
Of my cruel and hateful slaver who thought there was no used for fun;
           How I wish I had a gun.

And the hateful stinking waft rising on each heated draft
Killed me — filled me with a nauseous churning never felt before,
So that now, to still the sinking of my guts I stood there thinking,
"Will that lousy noisy trucker leave the quiet of my outhouse door?
Will he cease his racket, making worse what was bad enough before?
           For stench and noise I do deplore."

Presently the sound grew stronger; hesitating then no longer,
"Hey," said I, "you blasted scoundrel, that contraption has a roar
That would surely break my eardrums, rip and tear my tender eardrums,
Were it not for clouds of odor rising from my outhouse floor,
Stopping up my tender eardrums, " — here I opened wide the door;
           — Summer there, and nothing more."

Far into the outside peering, long I stood there, wondering, fearing,
Listening, and smelling smells no mortal ever had to smell before;
But there was no truck there; no noisy, rambling, drumming truck there;
And the dust upon the road moved not: the noise was unaccounted for.
Again I looked, and south for truck-sign, finding nothing as before;
           Hot dust there, and nothing more.

Back into the outhouse turning, eyes on fire and nostrils burning,
Soon again I heard the rambling somewhat louder than before;
"Good God," said I, and blessed my soul, for frightful sounds came from the hole;
Let me see, then what there at is, and this mystery explore
—Let my stomach turn a moment and this mystery explore;
                                    Or hold my ears forevermore."

Up I stood then full of wonder and peered into that blackness under;
And out there flopped a slimy chicken covered with ungodly mess;
Dripping brown and green and yellow, 'deed a most unsightly fellow;
Nowhere could you see the feathers that once had been his daily dress,
And the reeking, rancid odor from him made me like him all the less;
                                    The picture of unhappiness.

Then this putrid bird beguiling my great disgust into smiling,
By the sad forlorn decorum on the countenance it wore,
"By thy hopeless sad demeanor I would guess you never cleaner —
Ugly, smelling filthy chicken 'scaping from the depths beneath the door!"
                                Quoth the chicken, "Hell, what for?"

Much I marveled this ungainly fowl to hear discourse so plainly,
Though its answer nasty — and little chivalry it bore;
For we cannot help agreeing that no living human being
Ever yet was cursed with having bird upon his outhouse floor —
Reeking filthy rancid bird leaving sloppy messes on his outhouse floor
                              —With such a name as "Hell, what for?"

But the chicken, sitting dripping on the wooden floor kept quipping
That one phrase, as if his awful heart into that phrase he did outpour;
Nothing further then he uttered — not a heavy feather fluttered,
Till I scarcely more than muttered, "Other dreads have gone before;
If I'm lucky he will leave me, as bad things have left before."
                              Then the bird said, "Hell, what for?"

Startled by the stillness broken by reply so aptly spoken,
"Doubtless," said I, "what it utters is its only stock and store,
Caught from some unhappy owner who had been a constant loner,
Due to sad association with this denizen of such a core,
Till when asked to hope anew this beaten heart could only sigh and say once more,
                            'What's the use, man? Hell, what for?'"

But the chicken still beguiling my sore stomach into smiling,
Down I sat again reposing next to stinking bird upon the floor;
Then, upon the wood seat under, I began to question, wonder
What this dirty ugly slimy fiend covered with something kin to gore,
What this oozing, ghastly-smelling gaunt and grim mess upon the floor
Meant in croaking, "Hell, what for?"

This I sat engaged in guessing, but no syllable expressing
To the fowl whose slopping drippings now began to make eyes sore,
And wondered if my nostrils lost were worth the freedom from the boss,
And thought perhaps the stench could force me out to work some more;
Maybe, better judgment would tell my muscles to go and work some more
— Perish the thought, forevermore!

Then I smelt the air grow thicker; became my stomach even sicker
Than before, when I thought I was to drop from health no more.
"Wretch," I cried, "my boss hath sent thee — from the fumes below hath sent thee
As a conscience, hurtful conscience that I must go and work some more;
Leave me, out my outhouse, to my comics and rest still more!"
Quoth the chicken, "Hell, what for?"

"Prophet," said I, "thing of evil! — prophet still if bird or devil! —
Awful, ugly, and unholy wretch residing 'neath my outhouse floor,
Whether boss hath sent thee or bad luck unmerciful hath meant thee
To come so loudly and unwelcome from beneath my outhouse floor,
Tell me if the fates have reason to put me out to work some more!"
Quoth the chicken, "Hell, what for?"

"Prophet," said I, "thing of evil! — prophet still if bird or devil!
By the gas that boils below us round the substance we deplore;
Tell this soul with nausea churning if my way of life is turning,
And my lazy heart is burning truly to work as ne'er before!
If my soften muscles will come to hardness from working as ne'er before!"
Quoth the chicken, "Hell what for?"

"Be that phrase our sign of parting, bird or fiend!" I shrieked, upstarting
—"Get thee back into the oozing brown and yellow mass beneath my outhousef loor!
Take you asinine confusion and get back into seclusion!
Leave my outhouse clean and empty of thy horrid stenches by the score!
Take thy greasy form and push again into the mysterious darkness 'neath this floor!"
Quoth the chicken, "Hell, what for?"

And the chicken never slipping, still is dripping, still is dripping
On the rotten wooden boards that make my outhouse floor,
And the smell is worse than ever and my nose I'll have to sever,
For in my life I shall never exit from the outhouse door;
For that gas has gone from nose to head and boiled brain at very core
                            — And now it's blown — Forevermore!

The Forman Ranch at Knowlton

Made in the USA